BEHOLD

A GUIDED ADVENT JOURNAL FOR PRAYER AND MEDITATION

SR. MIRIAM JAMES HEIDLAND, SOLT

ILLUSTRATED BY JOSIAH HENLEY

AVE MARIA PRESS AVE Notre Dame, Indiana

Visit our website to find online components, including videos by Sr. Miriam James Heidland, SOLT, to enhance your experience with Behold this Advent. Go to https://www. avemariapress.com/private/page/behold-resources.

Nihil Obstat: Reverend Monsignor Michael Heintz, PhD
Censor Librorum
Imprimatur: Most Reverend Kevin C. Rhoades
Bishop of Fort Wayne–South Bend
Given at: Fort Wayne, Indiana, on 3 May 2022

Scripture quotations are from the *Revised Standard Version of the Bible—Second Catholic Edition (Ignatius Edition)*, copyright © 2006 National Council of the Churches of Christ in the United States of America. Used by permission. All rights reserved.

The English translation of Collects from *The Roman Missal* © 2010, International Commission on English in the Liturgy Corporation. All rights reserved.

O Antiphons excerpted from *Catholic Household Blessings and Prayers: Revised and Updated Edition* (Washington, DC: United States Conference of Catholic Bishops, 2020).

Founded in 1865, Ave Maria Press is a ministry of the United States Province of Holy Cross.

www.avemariapress.com

Paperback: ISBN-13 978-1-64680-194-7

E-book: ISBN-13 978-1-64680-195-4

Cover and interior images © 2022 Josiah Henley, heartofiesvs.etsy.com.

Cover and text design by Brianna Dombo.

Printed and bound in the United States of America.

CONTENTS

INTRODUCTION

JOURNEYING TO THE STABLE

The season of Advent conjures in us a distinct feeling of journey. Often that journey is one of frazzled haste and consumerism as we dash around to prepare our homes and meals for Christmas. Motivated by the desire to ensure our holiday is perfect, we can become swept away by the frenzy, and before we know it, Advent is behind us and Christmas Day is upon us. I want to invite you into a different experience this year. Together, let us set aside the material expectations of the world and instead dive into each day of our journey to approach the humble stable in Bethlehem.

Our life's journeys often take us to unexpected places, and the journey of Jesus, the King of kings and the Lord of lords, is certainly no exception. Jesus Christ comes to earth not in power and esteem but born of a humble woman. He is small, fragile, vulnerable. Rather than being born in the comfort and cleanliness of a well-lit home or the splendor of a castle, he is born in the poverty and dirt of a stable.

Jesus's circumstances are not coincidences but rather intentional movements of God, who wants to unite himself to us in every way, for Jesus is present in every stable of our lives. What we find in the stable where he is born are the same features that are present in our own lives: light and darkness, stench and freshness, beauty and sorrow.

Each of us comes into the world as a child. All of us have two parents. Sometimes these relationships are beautiful, sometimes they are broken, and they are almost always a mix of both. Yet somehow, in it all, the Lord comes to redeem, restore, and bring everything into wholeness and communion. Jesus is present in the stable of it all.

Advent, in a particular way, invites us to consider the restoration of the family. We see within our family lines the traces of the rupture of Adam and Eve. We see factions, divisions, loss, and sin. We ache for the restoration of marriages, children, grandchildren. We long for our families to bear the marks of the Holy Family: love, fidelity, joy, truth, safety, belonging, rest, peace. These longings are beautiful, dear friends. They are marks of eternity. The more we can allow God to heal us as children and parents, the more our families will take on the likeness of the Holy Family.

This Advent we will go on a journey with Mary, Joseph, the child Jesus, and the Holy Family. Each week we will spend time with one of the members of the Holy Family and experience the healing of motherhood, fatherhood, childhood, and family.

We will let them speak to us about our lives and our experiences of childhood and beyond so that Jesus can bring us into wholeness and communion. This journey will take you to places of your heart—some joyful, some tender. That is okay. The Holy Family is in no hurry to rush you along or coerce you into anything. They are simply present to be with you, to lead you into all truth.

As you reflect upon your earthly family and yourself as a child, God is with you. As you reflect upon Jesus, Mary, and Joseph as the Holy Family, God is with you. Nothing that happens within your heart is unknown to God. He is not surprised, nor is he dismayed. He has given you Mary and Joseph to be a real mother and father to you on this journey. Jesus is with you in every moment. Notice what happens within your heart these days, and bring everything to Jesus, Mary, and Joseph. They love you with unspeakable reverence and kindness.

May your heart be gently illumined during these days of light. May these days of Advent be a time of deep preparation for the birth of the Son of God—he who makes all things new—in your heart and life. May you find the Lord in every stable of your life and allow him to bring you home to the Father's house forever.

HOW TO USE
THIS JOURNAL

The *Behold* Advent journal combines daily meditations, questions for reflection, journaling space, prayers, and beautiful original art to draw you into a deeper, richer experience of Advent. It helps prepare you not only to experience the joy of Jesus's birth but also to journey with the Holy Family, to receive their healing love, to practice forgiveness and acceptance of your earthly family members, and to meet Jesus in the sacraments of Reconciliation and Holy Communion.

WHO IS *BEHOLD* FOR?

Behold is for anyone who desires to experience the Advent season as a healing journey that leads you to explore the crevices of your heart. The season of Advent is the ideal time to step back from your life and evaluate where you stand with God, yourself, and others. This Advent journal provides a daily path to prayer and reflection for healing and restoration.

Behold was designed for use in a group setting. There's something special about taking this Advent journey with a community, whether that community is your entire parish, a small group, or your family.

You can also use *Behold*'s meditations and journaling prompts on your own, to help you draw near to God, hear his voice in new ways, and pour out your heart to him as you turn your attention daily to the Holy Family's journey to Bethlehem. You may find that, this Advent, you're in special need of regular quiet times of connection with God; *Behold* is an excellent way to help you find that space each day.

HOW IS *BEHOLD* ORGANIZED?

Behold is organized into four parts:

✦ In part 1, you'll focus on receiving *Mary as your mother* and learning to trust her with your heart as you explore wounds from your relationship with your earthly mother. You'll close out the week with a prayer of thanksgiving and healing for your earthly mother.

✦ In part 2, you'll reflect on receiving *St. Joseph as your protector and father*. The meditations will help you unpack your experiences of fatherly love and help you regain trust in God the Father. The week closes with a prayer of thanksgiving and healing for your earthly father.

✦ In part 3, you'll focus on the *child Jesus* and reflect on your own childhood and childlike spirit. You'll rediscover the truth of your playfulness and tap into the simplicity of your inner child. You'll complete the week with a prayer of thanksgiving and healing for your childhood.

✦ In part 4, you'll deeply explore where your heart stands with God and how you can restore your understanding of *family* by accepting that no family, no individual, is perfect. You'll come to see this most fully on Christmas when Jesus comes to us humbly in imperfect circumstances to be born in our hearts.

Within each week, you'll encounter a simple daily pattern made up of the following parts:

✦ Each day opens with a *quotation* from a saint, a great teacher, or scripture in order to focus your thoughts on the key idea from that day's meditation.

✤ The *meditation* draws out a message from the liturgy, scripture, or the process of spiritual healing to help you experience the love of the Holy Family this Advent.

✤ The *reflection* challenges you to ponder and journal in response to the meditation, helping you identify practical ways to live out the Advent season more fully.

✤ Finally, after you've read and journaled, the closing *prayer* provides a starting point for your own requests and prayers of thanksgiving and praise to God.

In the final days of Advent, beginning on December 17, we begin the traditional "singing" of the O Antiphons. From the eighth century, the Church has heralded these antiphons during Vespers of the Divine Office before the singing of the Magnificat (Luke 1:46–55). Each antiphon, provided here with the reflections for the final days of Advent, is rich in proclamation of who Christ is, and the interrelating of the antiphons synthesizes the words from Revelation 12:20: "Come, Lord Jesus." I invite you on these days to allow each antiphon to wash over your heart in a particular way and draw you closer to Jesus in the detailed and personal fashion of his love for you. Proclaiming the truth of who God is, is healing. Whenever we proclaim his goodness, faithfulness, mercy, and wisdom, it brings us more deeply into wholeness and communion. What do you notice as you encounter each antiphon? What is each antiphon telling you about who Jesus is and who you are?

HOW SHOULD I READ *BEHOLD*?

This Advent journal's daily format is flexible enough to accommodate any reader's preferences: If you're a morning person, you may want to start your day with *Behold*, completing the entire day's reading, reflection, journaling, and prayer first thing in the morning. Or you may prefer to end your day by using *Behold* to focus your attention on Christ as you begin to rest from the day's activities. You may even decide to read and pray as a family in the morning and journal individually in the evening.

The key is finding what works for you, ensuring that you have time to read carefully, ponder deeply, write honestly, and connect intimately with the Lord in prayer.

Whatever approach you choose (and whether you decide to experience *Behold* with a group or on your own), be sure to visit https://www.avemariapress.com/private/page/behold-resources for extra resources to help you get the most out of this special Advent journey.

MARY IS NOT WEARIED WITH
OUR LITTLENESS; HER SMILE
COMES DOWN TO US LIKE A
BENEDICTION THROUGH THE
SEA OF FLICKERING CANDLES,
AND SHE BLESSES OUR WILD
FLOWERS WITHERING AT HER
FEET. FOR EACH ONE OF US IS
"ANOTHER CHRIST"; EACH ONE,
TO MARY, IS HER ONLY CHILD.
IT IS THEREFORE NOT TEDIOUS
TO HER TO HEAR THE TRIFLES
THAT WE TELL HER, TO LOOK AT
THE BRUISES THAT WE BRING TO
HER, AND SEEING OUR WOUND
OF SIN, TO HEAL IT.

CARYLL HOUSELANDER,
THE REED OF GOD

FIRST WEEK
OF ADVENT

MARY
AS HEALER

FIRST WEEK OF ADVENT

SUNDAY

TO YOU, O LORD, I LIFT UP MY
SOUL.
O MY GOD, IN YOU I TRUST,
LET ME NOT BE PUT TO
SHAME.

PSALM 25:1-2

SHE RECEIVES YOU

We begin the first week of our Advent season by meditating on our mothers, which is fitting because it is in our mothers that we find our beginning. Every human comes to earth through the womb of a woman, and that is made possible first and foremost by an act of receptivity. With Mary, we see her receive the message from the archangel Gabriel, who tells her she will conceive and bear a son through a virgin birth and become the mother of Jesus, the Son of God. Despite how startling this news must have been to Mary, a young girl on the brink of marriage to Joseph, she gives her fiat and is overshadowed by the Holy Spirit. At that moment, Jesus begins to be formed, just as you and I once did, in his mother's womb. Mary receives him without hesitation. So too does she receive us here and now.

Depending on the circumstances of how you were conceived and born, it may not be natural to image yourself as welcomed or happily received. This does not change the fact that in the quiet of your mother's womb, before she or your father knew you existed, *God began to form and shape you*. The Lord of lords willed you into existence, and Mary received you as her child just as your earthly mother received you in her body and heart. This is a profound and inscrutable reality of how you came to be in time, place, and circumstances.

No matter the situation of your beginnings, you are not an accident. You are chosen and beloved by God, and Mary has already received you into her heart. Although your mother may have had many different thoughts and emotions regarding your existence, Mary's heart for you is one of pure joy and delight. She can't wait to meet you. She already delights in you. She receives you.

REFLECT

What is the story of the beginning of your existence? What does Mary want to say to you in this story?

_____

_____

_____

_____

_____

_____

_____

_____

_____

_____

_____

_____

_____

_____

_____

_____

_____

_____

_____

_____

_____

_____

_____

_____

_____

_____

PRAY

_LOVING GOD, PLEASE HELP ME OPEN
MY HEART TO MARY'S MOTHERLY
PRESENCE AND YOUR GUIDING HAND
AS IT LEADS ME TO WHOLENESS._

FIRST WEEK OF ADVENT

MONDAY

BE STRONG, FEAR NOT!
BEHOLD, YOUR GOD
WILL COME WITH
VENGEANCE,
WITH THE RECOMPENSE OF
GOD.
HE WILL COME AND SAVE
YOU.

ISAIAH 35:4

I AM YOUR MOTHER

We now know that Mary has conceived us in her heart, in her womb. She tells St. Juan Diego, "Am I not here who am your Mother?" A child in the womb is fragile, defenseless, and dependent. At the same time, the mother's body holds the child within and quietly gives space and nurturing for the child to flourish, develop, and become. This is our state in Mary's heart. We are entirely vulnerable and yet perfectly nurtured and protected.

Your biological mother's womb offered you a similar haven: unseen, day and night, your mother's body nourished you and sustained you. God designed this process of human gestation to be perfect so that you would grow and thrive without restriction. True nurturing does not grasp at, take from, constrict, or smother. True nurturing feeds and protects, supports and encourages. True nurturing blesses.

Mary blesses you as her child. Her delight is to behold you, rejoice over you, and encourage you to grow toward everything Jesus has for you. We need not fear with Mary. She only gives and brings us to her son. But maybe when we think about being nurtured by a mother, we feel afraid and unseen, unprotected and underfed. It's likely that your earthly mother was not and is not perfect, and you have felt the effects of her deficiencies in some way.

We hear a lot about the "father wound," and for good reason. (We'll talk more about that one next week.) But we can also have a "mother wound," wherein our mother did not or does not provide for us in the way we need. We must ask Jesus to gently illumine the places in our hearts where our mothers have wounded us and where we are still bearing the pain of those wounds. Today we begin turning to Mary to tend to those wounds. We seek the healing power of her spouse, the Holy Spirit, to overcome us and be our life support.

REFLECT

What feelings rise up in you when you consider being nurtured by a mother? How has your earthly mother nurtured you? In what ways has your earthly mother fallen short? What kind of nurturing do you need from Mary now?

_____

_____

_____

_____

_____

_____

_____

_____

_____

_____

_____

_____

_____

_____

_____

_____

_____

_____

_____

_____

_____

_____

_____

_____

PRAY

*ALMIGHTY GOD, PLEASE HELP ME
TO TRUST IN MARY'S NURTURING
PROTECTION AS I BRING MY
WOUNDED HEART TO YOU TO BE
HEALED BY YOUR PERFECT LOVE.*

FIRST WEEK OF ADVENT

TUESDAY

ON THAT DAY THERE SHALL BE
NEITHER COLD NOR FROST. AND
THERE SHALL BE CONTINUOUS
DAY (IT IS KNOWN TO THE LORD),
NOT DAY AND NOT NIGHT, FOR
AT EVENING TIME THERE SHALL
BE LIGHT.

ZECHARIAH 14:7

TO GIVE TO THE LIGHT

A baby's arrival is most often met with great joy and anticipation. So much promise, so much hope, so much to be discovered: Who is this little person, and how will they change our hearts? How will the world be altered by this child's existence?

In some cultures, a variation of the Italian phrase *Dare alla Luce*, literally "to give to the light," is used to describe a woman giving birth. Each child is a light to this world, a light that has never before been seen by the world and that will never be seen again.

Mary receives us with this same joy: To her, you are a light—a stunning, sacred, and profound flame in her heart. This has been true from the day of your conception and throughout your development. As you grew in your mother's womb and revealed your presence to the world, Mary held you in her heart. As your mother's belly swelled, Mary watched over you. Others began to acknowledge your existence as a priceless treasure. Stories were told about you before you were even born. Your arrival and the light you would be was joyfully anticipated

Mary rejoices in and over the light that you are to this world. She does not compare you to her other children. She sees all of you at once and loves every facet of your being. She knows every unique crevice of your heart and revels in your existence. You bring her joy. Your mother delights in you.

REFLECT

How do you perceive being a light to this world? What does Mary want to say to you in this?

_____

_____

_____

_____

_____

_____

_____

_____

_____

_____

_____

_____

_____

_____

_____

_____

_____

_____

_____

_____

_____

_____

_____

_____

PRAY

_MARY, PLEASE PRAY FOR ME, THAT
I MAY SEE AND BE THE LIGHT GOD
INTENDED FOR ME TO BE IN THIS
WORLD._

WEDNESDAY

IF IT SEEM SLOW, WAIT FOR IT;
IT WILL SURELY COME,
IT WILL NOT DELAY.

HABAKKUK 2:3

TUNED IN

In the first minutes after a baby is born, the child searches for connection with his mother. He longs to be reminded of his attachment and to feel protected. We all come into this world looking for someone looking for us. The desire to be seen, found, noticed, and cared for is not something we "grow out of," even if the contours of that desire change as we mature. We all desire to have someone attuned to our needs. Every single one of us needed, and still needs in ways, someone who truly sees us, understands us, and knows the ways of our heart.

A mother knows her child and is attuned and attentive to the movements of her child's heart, mind, body, and soul. In his writings, St. John Paul II reminds us that women bear the unique gift of receiving others in heart and body, and God has given them a particular gift of intuition and attunement to bring the other person into harmony, sympathetic relationship, safety, and communion. We see this in how a mother can distinguish between her child's cries of hunger or anger and between a laugh from fear or delight. Many times, only a mother can quiet her restless child. Her voice, her scent, her arms are the only place a child will rest and find safety and refuge.

Spiritually, Mary is our mother and is attuned to our every need. She hears and sees us and our deepest wounds. She desires to bring us into her heart and to carry us to the Lord. We need only to trust her with this task—to trust that she is attentive to our needs and waiting to receive us.

REFLECT

Where is a particular place in your heart that you need to experience the Lord's care and attunement? What does Mary want to say to you in this?

_____

_____

_____

_____

_____

_____

_____

_____

_____

_____

_____

_____

_____

_____

_____

_____

_____

_____

_____

_____

_____

_____

_____

_____

_____

_____

PRAY

*MOTHER MARY, PLEASE HEAR AND
SEE ME AND MY DEEPEST WOUNDS.
PLEASE TAKE ME INTO YOUR HEART
AND CARRY ME TO THE LORD.*

FIRST WEEK OF ADVENT

THURSDAY

BUT YOU ARE NEAR, O LORD,
AND ALL YOUR
COMMANDMENTS
ARE TRUE.

PSALM 119:151

A STEADFAST LOVE

Our hearts desire and are made for steadfast love—a love that is unwavering and dutifully firm. Steadfast love is not limited to perfect circumstances, and neither is God. God's love is warm, safe, strong, secure, unconditional, faithful, and all-encompassing. God's love is continual and ever-unfolding. Our hearts are made for a bond of love that is eternal, that never ends. This is true and authentic love. We see this love in a particularly feminine and maternal way in Mary.

From the moment of your conception, your mother is biologically your mother every day hence. She is your mother in season and out of season, in joy and in sorrow, in sickness and in health. In the divine mystery of God, this woman God chose to be your mother remains through it all. Perhaps she was unable to be present to you in many ways throughout your life, yet the establishment of her motherhood remains. Our ability to acknowledge this reality—that we have a biological mother who has played a significant role in forming our understanding of faithfulness— is essential to accessing the love that Mary offers us.

Although Mary is not our biological mother, her spiritual motherhood is real and knows no bounds. In her son she has chosen us in steadfast love, and her love does not fail us. Mary is strong, secure, steady, and faithful. Her face is always toward us. She is not fearful, avoidant, or anxious about the places in our hearts that are painful or shame inducing. Even though we constantly doubt our worthiness, Mary has been given to us by Jesus despite ourselves. She remains given in deep love and care forever.

REFLECT

What is your experience of maternal steadfast love? In what ways do you feel unworthy of Mary's love?

_____

_____

_____

_____

_____

_____

_____

_____

_____

_____

_____

_____

_____

_____

_____

_____

_____

_____

_____

_____

_____

_____

_____

_____

PRAY

_O GOD, IN YOUR LOVE I FEEL WARM,
SAFE, AND SECURE, DESPITE MY
EARTHLY CHALLENGES. THANK YOU
FOR YOUR STEADFAST LOVE._

FIRST WEEK OF ADVENT

FRIDAY

WAIT FOR THE LORD;
BE STRONG, AND LET YOUR
HEART TAKE COURAGE;
YES, WAIT FOR THE LORD!

PSALM 27:14

THE TRUTH OF
YOUR EARTHLY MOTHER

On Friday of this first week of Advent, you may have noticed some places of pain in your heart regarding your earthly mother. You may know some sorrowful stories about yourself and about your mother that did not include tenderness, attunement, receptivity, joy, or steadfast love. You may not even know your mother, or perhaps you wish that God would have given you someone else. Maybe your mother had many other children to attend to, or maybe you felt like she never quite understood you or attended to the cares and concerns of your life. Maybe you're like me—you are adopted. Perhaps you adore your mother; you think the world of her and wish that everyone had a mother just like yours.

Whatever your circumstances, Mary understands all these places in your heart. She knows that our mothers have gifts and beauty. She also knows that our mothers are not perfect, that in their own weakness and brokenness they most likely hurt us sometime in our lives. Mary is understanding and receptive of all these moments. She knows it can be hard to face these places in truth and forgiveness of heart.

On this Friday, Mary would love to share with you about your mother and the truth of your mother's heart. She wants to open your mind and heart to your past and present relationship with your earthly mother. She wants to give you the gift of understanding. Would you allow Mary to be with you here today and reveal to you whatever she would like to reveal? Mary reveals these places with gentleness and the wisdom of God's love. May we allow her to speak to our hearts.

REFLECT

What is Mary revealing to you about your earthly mother? What truths are harder to open your mind and heart to than others, and why do you think that is? How might you begin the healing process of forgiveness concerning these truths?

_____

_____

_____

_____

_____

_____

_____

_____

_____

_____

_____

_____

_____

_____

_____

_____

_____

_____

_____

_____

_____

_____

_____

PRAY

*JESUS, GRANT ME AN OPEN MIND
AND AN OPEN HEART, THAT I MAY
COME TO UNDERSTAND THE
TRUTH OF MY EARTHLY MOTHER'S
HEART AND KNOW THE WISDOM OF
GOD'S LOVE.*

FIRST WEEK OF ADVENT

SATURDAY

IN THE DAY WHEN THE LORD
BINDS UP THE HURT OF HIS
PEOPLE, AND HEALS THE WOUNDS
INFLICTED BY HIS BLOW.

ISAIAH 30:26

THANKSGIVING AND HEALING FOR OUR MOTHERS

God, thank you for the gift of my mother. Thank you for your eternal mystery of bringing me to life in her womb. Thank you for her yes of receiving me and giving light to this world. In her womb I was fearfully and wonderfully made, and I thank you for this, Lord. Thank you for the ways my mother was attuned, caring, and nurturing to me. Thank you for the gift that she was and is to me.

I also pray for healing for my mother and for myself in the places where she has hurt me. For the times when she was not tender, kind, steadfast, or loving, please heal me, Lord.

Please heal me from any bitterness that I may have toward my mother. (*Ask the Holy Spirit to bring to mind any resentments or judgments you may have toward your mother or any areas of unforgiveness.*) Lord, help me to be honest about these places and release these places to you, surrendering the outcome to you, knowing that you make all things new.

God, our Father, bless us in your love as your precious children. Jesus, please cleanse my mother and myself in your precious blood, healing our hearts and strengthening our love of you. Holy Spirit, may your healing love come upon us both at this very moment.

Mary, may I receive you anew as my mother. Open my heart with your gentle care. Show me how to love as you love, and set me free in the heart of your son, in the joy that never ends.

Amen.

REFLECT

For what are you especially grateful regarding your mother? What are some resentments or judgments you may have toward your mother or any areas of unforgiveness that you would like the Holy Spirit to help you with?

_____

_____

_____

_____

_____

_____

_____

_____

_____

_____

_____

_____

_____

_____

_____

_____

_____

_____

_____

_____

PRAY

*DEAR GOD, FOR THE GIFT OF
MY LIFE AND THE WAYS THAT MY
MOTHER WAS ATTUNED, CARING, AND
NURTURING TO ME—THANK YOU.
IN THE PLACES WHERE SHE HAS
HURT ME—PLEASE HELP ME
RELEASE THESE PLACES TO YOU,
SURRENDERING THE OUTCOME TO
YOU, KNOWING THAT YOU MAKE ALL
THINGS NEW.*

AS WE PLACE OURSELVES IN
THE POSITION OF JESUS IN ST.
JOSEPH'S ARMS, WE CAN LEARN
THE GREATEST EXPERIENCE OF
FATHERHOOD. WE LEARN FROM
ST. JOSEPH WHAT IT MEANS TO
BE UNCONDITIONALLY LOVED. IT
IS AN INVITATION TO BE LITTLE
AND CHILDLIKE, AND WHEN
WE TAKE THE RISK OF BEING
VULNERABLE LIKE A CHILD, WE
GET A TASTE OF DIVINE LOVE
AND WE EXPERIENCE A FATHER'S
TENDERNESS FOR HIS SON.

FR. BONIFACE HICKS,
THROUGH THE HEART OF ST. JOSEPH

SECOND WEEK
OF ADVENT

JOSEPH AS PROTECTOR

SECOND WEEK OF ADVENT

SUNDAY

YES, O PEOPLE IN ZION WHO
DWELL AT JERUSALEM; YOU
SHALL WEEP NO MORE. . . .
AND THE LORD WILL CAUSE HIS
MAJESTIC VOICE TO BE HEARD.

ISAIAH 30:19, 30

AN IRREPLACEABLE FIGURE

We continue our Advent journey in the second week with meditations on fathers. A father is an irreplaceable figure in a child's life with gifts that only a father can give. A father gifts himself to the mother and, through the blessing of God, a child is conceived. Half of your DNA comes from your mother and the other half comes from your father. Although you were carried in the womb of your mother and have an immediate bond with her, your father's presence through his gift of self and the strong affirmation he brings is the complementary counterpart in the symphony of your creation and flourishing.

Here we see the stunning gift of St. Joseph. Though not the biological father of Jesus, Joseph is chosen by God to help unfold, guide, and protect the humanity of Jesus. Joseph's presence, preceded through the bond of loving betrothal to Mary, is a stable and guiding force in Jesus's life. Joseph is present to Jesus throughout Mary's pregnancy and actively anticipates and prepares for his arrival.

As Mary is a mother to Jesus and to you, so Joseph is a father to Jesus and to you. He desires to be present to you to help unfold, guide, and protect your humanity. Joseph is not a passive bystander but a powerful witness of the providence and presence of God.

REFLECT

What is your experience of a father's presence in your life since you were a child in the womb until now? What does Joseph want to say to you in this?

_____

_____

_____

_____

_____

_____

_____

_____

_____

_____

PRAY

_ST. JOSEPH, PRAY FOR ME, THAT
I WILL KNOW YOUR STABLE AND
GUIDING PRESENCE IN MY LIFE AND
AS I ANTICIPATE AND PREPARE FOR
THE LORD'S ARRIVAL THIS WEEK OF
ADVENT._

SECOND WEEK OF ADVENT

MONDAY

STRENGTHEN THE WEAK HANDS,
AND MAKE FIRM THE
FEEBLE KNEES.

ISAIAH 35:3

TRUE STRENGTH

When we call to mind the idea of masculine strength, we often think of a domineering or distant presence—one that is destructive, detached, and cold. We can look to St. Joseph to show us the masculine gift of true strength. Joseph's strong, steady, and loving presence gives Jesus the safety he needs to grow, mature, and learn. Rather than forcing a process or insisting on his own way, Joseph creates a space for Jesus to grow into the fullness of who he is. In doing so, he models true strength for us.

True strength allows for others to rest in the safety of protection and care. It gently orders chaos and generously brings life. When we are in the presence of true strength, our hearts can relax and expand, unhindered by fear of rejection. We know that we do not have to be afraid, nor will we be deceived or taken advantage of. This safety allows us to heal, grow, feel joy, and experience new life. St. Joseph offers us these feelings of safety, no matter what burdens or wounds we carry.

When a father attends to his child and brings safety with his strength, the child comes to know the truth of their value and worth as a beloved child of God to whom the Father always attends. A father brings safety in the strength of who he is for his child.

Joseph brings to you the safety of his strength. His loving care for you heals wounds caused by the misuse of strength and the places where safety has been broken. The love of Joseph strengthens our hearts and guides our lives.

REFLECT

How do you see the masculine gift of safety in strength? How have you been wounded by the misuse of strength?

_____

_____

_____

_____

_____

_____

_____

_____

_____

_____

_____

_____

_____

_____

_____

_____

_____

_____

_____

_____

_____

_____

_____

_____

PRAY

*ALMIGHTY FATHER, AWAKEN MY
SENSE OF YOUR TRUE STRENGTH IN
WHICH I CAN HEAL, GROW, FEEL JOY,
AND EXPERIENCE NEW LIFE AS YOUR
BELOVED CHILD.*

SECOND WEEK OF ADVENT

TUESDAY

THE GRASS WITHERS, THE
FLOWER FADES;
BUT THE WORD OF OUR
GOD WILL STAND FOR
EVER.

ISAIAH 40:8

PERSEVERING
THROUGH MYSTERY

We see St. Joseph as a faithful, loving husband and father through all the ups and downs of life. We see him faithful and loving as he hears the news of Jesus's existence in the womb of Mary through the overshadowing of the Holy Spirit. We see him faithful and loving as he leads his beautiful, pregnant wife on a donkey to Bethlehem. We see him faithful and loving as he searches for a safe place for her to give birth. We see him faithful and loving as he heeds the urgency of a message in a dream and takes his wife and son to Egypt to escape Herod's murderous wrath. We see him faithful and loving as he and Mary search for Jesus, only to astonishingly find him in the Temple sitting among the teachers, listening to them and asking them questions. St. Joseph perseveres through all the mysteries of life in fidelity and love.

The beauty of a father's fidelity and love to those in his care roots and grounds them in secure love. When a father perseveres and remains faithful, even at great cost to himself, a child learns that love is unconditional and all-encompassing. In this witness a child receives the message that they are worth fighting for, protecting, pursuing, showing up for—no matter what.

God the Father has loved you in this exact way since your conception, and he has given us the life of St. Joseph to illustrate this paternal love and perseverance played out in the practical actions and gestures of a father. It's highly unlikely that your earthly father lived as perfectly as St. Joseph, or that he exemplified perseverance in a way that made you feel constantly secure. But that doesn't mean you are left without an understanding of what it means to be loved by a true father. St. Joseph, together with God the Father, watches over you and is faithful to you.

REFLECT

Where do you need the gift of masculine perseverance in your life today? How have you experienced masculine perseverance in the past?

_____

_____

_____

_____

_____

_____

_____

_____

_____

_____

_____

_____

_____

_____

_____

_____

_____

_____

_____

_____

_____

_____

PRAY

_DEAR GOD, AS ST. JOSEPH WAS A
FAITHFUL, LOVING HUSBAND AND
FATHER THROUGH EXTRAORDINARY
CHALLENGES, MAY I PERSEVERE
THROUGH ALL THE MYSTERIES OF
LIFE IN MY FAITHFULNESS AND LOVE
FOR YOU._

SECOND WEEK OF ADVENT

WEDNESDAY

COME TO ME, ALL WHO LABOR
AND ARE HEAVY LADEN, AND I
WILL GIVE YOU REST.

MATTHEW 11:28

A TENDER FATHER

Our experience of father figures throughout our lives—in the form of biological fathers as well as men who supported us, such as teachers, coaches, mentors, and so on—drastically shapes how we understand God's temperament. When we haven't witnessed a man who is emotionally mature and able to convey his warmth and affection, it can be difficult to see God as a loving Father.

The challenge lies in part with the culture of machismo, in which the archetypal male is impenetrable and unapologetic. To experience the tenderness and warmth of God the Father, we must move beyond a superficial understanding of masculine strength and recognize the gift of a man who speaks and acts with tenderness.

Tenderness is not weakness, an absence of strength. Quite the contrary. True tenderness is strength under control. It is channeled strength in kindness to hear the heart of another and move toward the person in life-giving love, concern, and care. The truth spoken in kindness has the power to unlock hardened hearts, heal shame, and bring new life. We see in the gospels how tender Jesus is with sinners. Many times, I am sure, the inflections in his voice and the mannerisms of his movements bore the hallmark of St. Joseph and his loving care.

When a father encounters his child with tenderness, their heart receives him. When a father channels his strength and necessary correction of his child with firm tenderness, he accesses a part of their heart that is missed and often crushed in harshness. When a father approaches the painful places of his child's heart with tenderness, it gives safety for the truth to come out and for restoration to take place. Tenderness interrupts the cycle of fear, self-hatred, and shame and gives way for healing and repair.

St. Joseph is tender with the vulnerable places of our hearts and lives. He would love to speak to you about those places if you would allow him to do so.

REFLECT

What does St. Joseph want to reveal to you today about the gift of a father's tenderness in your life? In what ways have you experienced God the Father's love through the father figures in your life?

_____

_____

_____

_____

_____

_____

_____

_____

_____

_____

_____

_____

_____

_____

_____

_____

_____

_____

_____

_____

_____

_____

PRAY

_DEAR GOD, HELP ME OPEN TO THE
EXPERIENCE OF YOUR TENDERNESS
AND WARMTH SO THAT IT MAY
UNHARDEN MY HEART, HEAL MY
SHAME, AND BRING ME NEW LIFE._

SECOND WEEK OF ADVENT

THURSDAY

THE LORD IS GRACIOUS AND
MERCIFUL,
SLOW TO ANGER AND
ABOUNDING IN MERCY.

PSALM 145:8

HONOR AND HONESTY

Throughout his life, we see that St. Joseph is a man of great honor and honesty. These two characteristics are at the foundation of any great man. When a man lives in and with honor and honesty, the greatness of his character shines through and blesses everyone around him.

We see the honor and honesty of St. Joseph as he discovers Mary's pregnancy during their betrothal. We see him honoring and in honesty of the law and honoring and in honesty of his future wife. Even though it could have been "easier" for Joseph to leave Mary, he does not take the easy path and shrink from the law nor the love he has for Mary. In his honor and honesty, Joseph receives the Lord's message and plan during a dream.

We've all had moments when it seems as if it would be "easier" to disregard or disrespect the law. There are also times when it seems as if it would be "easier" to shy away from a hard conversation or shy away from the truth of what we need to do or say. Yet when we act in and with honor and honesty, it opens our hearts to hear the Lord and to receive strength and illumination from the Lord, even if it seems difficult and arduous. When a father rises to the occasion and accepts his purpose to live with honor and honesty, it drastically blesses his family, just as St. Joseph's actions blessed Mary and Jesus. This witness allows his child to see that living in the truth is healing and gives great strength, firmness, and clarity of purpose.

REFLECT

When do you feel like taking the "easier" path instead of the honorable and honest one? What about St. Joseph's honor and honesty inspires you to make sound decisions?

_____

_____

_____

_____

_____

_____

_____

_____

_____

_____

_____

_____

_____

_____

_____

_____

_____

_____

_____

_____

_____

_____

_____

PRAY

_GOD, STRENGTHEN MY SPIRIT, THAT
I MAY RISE TO MEET MY PURPOSE TO
LIVE WITH HONOR AND HONESTY,
EVEN WHEN IT SEEMS DIFFICULT. ON
EVERY OCCASION, HELP ME CHOOSE
THE PATH THAT LEADS TO YOU._

SECOND WEEK OF ADVENT

FRIDAY

I AM THE LIGHT OF THE WORLD;
HE WHO FOLLOWS ME WILL NOT
WALK IN DARKNESS, BUT WILL
HAVE THE LIGHT OF LIFE.

JOHN 8:12

THE TRUTH OF
YOUR FATHER'S HEART

As we come once again to Friday, you may have noticed some places of pain in your heart this week regarding your earthly father. Perhaps your father was marginally present in your life, either physically or emotionally, or perhaps you do not even know who he is. Maybe your father displayed broken manifestations of strength that caused your heart to hide and close rather than open and rest. Maybe your father was tender in some ways but lacked honor, honesty, or true strength in how he interacted with you and others. Or perhaps you can see the immense goodness of your father and the wonderful man that he was/is, but you have noticed some places of sorrow and tenderness in your heart as your father could not be everything at all times to you. I gently invite you once again to the truth that noticing these realities is okay and God is not offended by any of them.

If we embrace the humility that St. Joseph models, we can bring everything. St. Joseph can hear our deepest praise of our fathers and our deepest sorrows. St. Joseph can bear our pain from lack of affection, death, or divorce in our families. He is with us as a man, a father, and a saint who knew difficulty in every way. It is his desire to intercede for the healing of our hearts regarding our relationships with our fathers and to also be a true spiritual father to us now. On this Friday, St. Joseph desires to share with you about your father and the truth of your father's heart.

REFLECT

How can you welcome St. Joseph's presence into your life today?
What might you want to share about your earthly father with St.
Joseph, your spiritual father?

_____

_____

_____

_____

_____

_____

_____

_____

_____

_____

_____

_____

PRAY

*GOOD ST. JOSEPH, YOU REMIND ME
OF THE TENDERNESS AND FIDELITY
OF GOD'S LOVE. I OPEN MY HEART
TO YOUR VOICE.*

SECOND WEEK OF ADVENT

SATURDAY

YOU WHO ARE READY AT THE
APPOINTED TIME, IT IS
WRITTEN,
TO CALM THE WRATH OF
GOD BEFORE IT BREAKS
OUT IN FURY,
TO TURN THE HEART OF THE
FATHER TO THE SON,
AND TO RESTORE THE
TRIBES OF JACOB.

SIRACH 48:10

THANKSGIVING AND HEALING FOR OUR FATHERS

God, thank you for the gift of my father. Thank you for your eternal mystery of bringing me to life through his gift. Thank you for the ways he has been a strong affirmation in life and a reflection of your love, fidelity, truth, and protection. Thank you for the gift that he was and is to me.

I also pray for healing for my father and for myself in the places where he has hurt me. For the times when he was not present, kind, or pursuing of my heart, please heal me, Lord.

Please heal me from any bitterness that I may have toward my father. (*Ask the Holy Spirit to bring to mind any resentments or judgments you may have toward your father or any areas of unforgiveness.*) Lord, help me to be honest about these places and release these places to you, surrendering the outcome to you, knowing that you make all things new.

God, our Father, bless us in your love as your precious children. Jesus, please cleanse my father and myself in your precious blood, healing our hearts and strengthening our love of you. Holy Spirit, may your healing love come upon us both at this very moment.

St. Joseph, may I receive you anew as my father. Open my heart with your gentle care. Show me how to love as you love, and set me free in the heart of your son, in the joy that never ends.

Amen.

REFLECT

For what are you especially grateful regarding your father? What are some resentments or judgments you may have toward your father or any areas of unforgiveness that you would like the Holy Spirit to help you with? How might reflecting on St. Joseph's difficulties help you find forgiveness for your earthly father?

_____

_____

_____

_____

_____

_____

_____

_____

_____

_____

_____

_____

_____

_____

_____

_____

_____

_____

_____

_____

PRAY

*DEAR GOD, FOR THE GIFT OF MY LIFE
AND THE WAYS THAT MY FATHER HAS
BEEN A STRONG AFFIRMATION IN LIFE
AND A REFLECTION OF YOUR LOVE,
FIDELITY, TRUTH, AND PROTECTION—
THANK YOU. IN THE PLACES WHERE
HE HAS HURT ME—PLEASE HELP ME
RELEASE THESE PLACES TO YOU,
SURRENDERING THE OUTCOME TO
YOU, KNOWING THAT YOU MAKE ALL
THINGS NEW.*

THE HUMAN HEART IS ALWAYS
FILLED WITH SOME KIND OF
WONDER. IT IS ONE OF THE
FIRST SIGNS OF THE GROWING
AWARENESS OF A SMALL CHILD.
WHO HAS NOT SMILED TO SEE
A LITTLE INFANT DISCOVERING
THAT HE HAS FEET, HE HAS
HANDS! HE IS FULL OF WONDER!
THEN, AS HE GROWS HE BECOMES
MORE AND MORE FULL OF
WONDER AT THE THINGS HE CAN
DO. WONDER IS SO RADICAL TO
THE HUMAN HEART.

MOTHER MARY FRANCIS, PCC,
*COME, LORD JESUS: MEDITATIONS
ON THE ART OF WAITING*

THIRD WEEK
OF ADVENT

THE CHILD
JESUS

THIRD WEEK OF ADVENT

GAUDETE SUNDAY

O GOD, WHO SEE HOW YOUR
PEOPLE FAITHFULLY AWAIT THE
FEAST OF THE LORD'S NATIVITY,
ENABLE US, WE PRAY, TO ATTAIN
THE JOYS OF SO GREAT A
SALVATION AND TO CELEBRATE
THEM ALWAYS WITH SOLEMN
WORSHIP AND GLAD REJOICING.

COLLECT FOR MASS OF THE DAY

A SPIRIT OF WONDER

We delightfully enter into the third week of Advent with meditations on being a child and childhood. How fitting that today we light the third candle on the Advent wreath. This candle, which is unlike the rest, is rose in color and signifies joy and gladness at the proximate arrival of a child who changed the entire course of humanity. It also symbolizes the joy in the hearts of Mary and Elizabeth as they shared in the beautiful connection of being miraculously pregnant with boys who would change the course of human history.

We are in awe of this miracle: that the Son of God, the King and Lord of the universe, comes to earth as a small, defenseless child. God's plans are gloriously unlike our own, and they have so much to teach us about how he loves us.

Jesus loves us so deeply and so entirely that he takes on every aspect of our lives and unites it to himself. He, too, was conceived in the womb of a woman. He, too, was fashioned in secret for nine months before entering into this world. He, too, was dependent as he nursed, cried, ate, slept, had his diaper changed, and learned how to talk and walk. He, too, lived in a spirit of wonder as he discovered the world in his human nature. We can imagine that he loved fresh air, twinkling lamp lights, and animals, just as all young children do. The humility and innocence of Jesus is so stunningly lovely just as it was in you as you toddled around and delighted your parents.

Jesus does not fear the experience of innocence and littleness; rather, he takes it upon himself and delights in it.

REFLECT

Do you remember moments of wonder and joy as a child? What are some of your favorite childhood memories? What does Jesus want to say to you and show you in this?

PRAY

LORD JESUS, HELP ME DROP MY DEFENSES, THAT I MAY LIVE WITH A CHILDLIKE SPIRIT OF WONDER AND TAKE DELIGHT IN ALL OF GOD'S CREATION.

THIRD WEEK OF ADVENT

MONDAY

MAKE ME TO KNOW YOUR WAYS,
O LORD;
TEACH ME YOUR PATHS.

PSALM 25:4

A PLAYFUL SPIRIT

"Do you want to play?" is probably one of the most common phrases uttered by children. Children love to play. Far from being a frivolous exercise of time wasting, play is how children discover the world and learn about themselves and others. Play teaches many things, including the beauty of imagination and freedom of heart. Who of us as a child has not conquered imaginary lands, slayed the largest dragons, or held the most enchanting tea parties replete with lace dresses and stuffed bears as guests? Play opens our hearts, allowing us to dream without restraint as we test those dreams against the rules of reality.

Play teaches us about others as we push and pull against the rules of a game and the fairness with which we regard another. Play teaches us that we do not always win or get to be the star of a show but that everyone has a necessary part in their role of life. Play teaches us how to navigate, negotiate, and bring into harmony. Play is a very important invitation, and we don't ever grow out of it.

Jesus played as a boy, as all boys do, and he would have retained that playful heart as he grew into manhood, navigating the beauty of life and the many relationships he had. I am sure he played with the children who accompanied their parents on the journey of discipleship. And I am sure there were many nights by the fire with his disciples that held much laughter, jokes, and games. So human Jesus is. Perhaps he is inviting us all to learn how to play again.

Being playful as an adult isn't always easy to imagine because of how seriously we tend to take ourselves. But playfulness can look many ways depending on your personality and interests. In many cases, you can exercise your playfulness through creative endeavors, such as art or handworks. You could also take some time to enjoy creation, an athletic event, or some quality time with a dear friend or family member. Perhaps the least amount of effort is to take time each day to decompress and pray for the gift of a playful spirit.

REFLECT

What is your experience of play as a child and now? What are ways you connect with and express your playfulness today? What does Jesus want to say to you in this?

_____

_____

_____

_____

_____

_____

_____

_____

_____

_____

_____

_____

PRAY

*JESUS, THANK YOU FOR THE
INVITATION TO RECLAIM A PLAYFUL
SPIRIT. PLEASE GUIDE ME TO
EXERCISE MY PLAYFULNESS WITH
HUMILITY, FAIRNESS, AND A HEALING
SENSE OF HUMOR.*

75

THIRD WEEK OF ADVENT

TUESDAY

FOR I WILL LEAVE IN THE MIDST
OF YOU
A PEOPLE HUMBLE AND
LOWLY.
THEY SHALL SEEK REFUGE IN THE
NAME OF THE LORD.

ZEPHANIAH 3:12

AN INVITATION
TO OPENNESS

We see the deep openness of Jesus as an infant, as a child. The Son of God comes to us humble and lowly, receptive and docile, yet strong in the Father's pure gift of love. In Jesus we find no self-defense mechanisms, no hardness of heart, and no coercion. There is no compulsion, manipulation, or threats. There is only openness, light, and invitation to communion. He desires nothing for himself. He wants only your eternal happiness.

Of the child Jesus, St. Thérèse is quoted as saying, "I cannot fear a God who made himself so small for me . . . I love him! He is, in fact, nothing but love and mercy." The smallness of Jesus as an infant and the beauty of his heart therein is an invitation to be open to receive him, to receive love, to give love, to receive the gift of ourselves in him.

We often fear our smallness and openness and blame those characteristics and those parts of ourselves for our pain and life's betrayals. When we do that, we spend the rest of our lives avoiding anything or anyone who touches upon those places, and we live in fear and self-protection. Jesus is showing us another way—a freer way.

Think back to when you were a child—your openness, docility, and dependency were beautiful things. They still are. Consider how you can tap into your childlike heart to foster a spirit of deeper vulnerability.

How do you feel about being totally open, docile, and small? Try to recall a time from your childhood when your vulnerability was delighted in, then describe how it felt to be affirmed in your openness.

_____

_____

_____

_____

_____

_____

_____

_____

_____

_____

_____

_____

_____

_____

_____

_____

_____

_____

_____

_____

_____

_____

_____

_____

_____

_____

_____

PRAY

_O GOD, BREAK DOWN THE BARRIERS
OF MY HARDENED HEART, THAT I
MAY FREELY RECEIVE YOUR PURE
GIFT OF LOVE._

THIRD WEEK OF ADVENT

WEDNESDAY

GRANT WE PRAY, ALMIGHTY GOD,
THAT THE COMING SOLEMNITY
OF YOUR SON MAY BESTOW
HEALING UPON US IN THIS
PRESENT LIFE AND BRING US THE
REWARDS OF LIFE ETERNAL.

COLLECT FOR MASS OF THE DAY

SAFE TO REST

We can imagine the tender gaze and careful watchfulness of Mary and Joseph as Jesus sleeps calmly in the dark of night. We can feel Mary's and Joseph's constant concern for their only child and their dreams for his future. Even before Jesus is born, as the Holy Family journeys to Bethlehem with the future unknown, we can sense the protective hand of Mary upon her womb while Joseph surrounds them both with his careful attentiveness to their surroundings. In the care of Mary and Joseph, young Jesus was safe to rest. He was safe to develop and become all he was intended to be. He was safe to grow into the man who was destined to change the world.

The same principles apply to us: When we sense that we are physically and emotionally safe, we feel free to develop, heal, commune, express, and rest. When a child feels safe, the child can express all that is in their heart, knowing it will be received and that love and wisdom will be returned to them. Safety allows for our bodies to function properly and for our hearts and minds to bond in secure love rather than fear.

This freedom contrasts starkly with the way we cinch up and guard our hearts when the threat of rejection or abandonment approaches. When doubts about our dignity creep into our hearts and minds, we become frozen and numb, unable to feel the warmth of love from another person or from God. We must practice the habit of resting in the safety of God, trusting in his fatherly protection in the same way Jesus trusted in Mary and Joseph.

Recall some places where you found safety as a child and some of your fears as a child. Consider where you find safety now as an adult. Consider where in your life it does not seem safe enough to let your guard down and be seen and loved there. Consider that Jesus is with you in every moment of your life.

REFLECT

What were some of your fears as a child? Where did you find safety? What does Jesus want to say to you in these places, and what does he want to show you about the safety of his love?

_____

_____

_____

_____

_____

_____

_____

_____

_____

_____

_____

_____

_____

_____

_____

_____

_____

_____

_____

_____

_____

_____

_____

_____

_____

PRAY

*ALMIGHTY GOD, I REST IN YOUR SAFE
EMBRACE. I TRUST IN THE WARMTH
OF YOUR LOVE TO THAW THE FROZEN
PLACES IN MY HEART.*

THIRD WEEK OF ADVENT

THURSDAY

PREPARE THE WAY OF THE LORD,
MAKE HIS PATHS STRAIGHT.

LUKE 3:4

TIME TO GROW

Growth is truly a wonderous mystery of God. Our whole life is about growth in every way. Even Jesus grew, as the Gospel of Luke 2:52 beautifully reveals: "And Jesus increased [grew] in wisdom and in stature, and in favor with God and man." Growth is a necessity, and it is good that we grow. It is good that we mature, develop, learn, and increase.

Perhaps some of our most painful places in life are where we feel "stuck." Sometimes we feel stuck in emotional or relational patterns. Maybe we feel stuck in an addiction or in a situation at work that seems hopeless and we feel powerless to change anything about it. Feeling stuck—without the seeming possibility of growth, resolution, or a way out—can be deeply demoralizing, and it robs us of joy, wonder, and the ability to see what is true.

In these places, Jesus would like to show us something. Although we might find that we are facing an unsurmountable or overwhelming situation, with Jesus there is always a way through. Jesus is the way, the truth, and the life (see John 14:6) With him, there is always a way through whatever we are facing. The Lord knows our paths, and he desires to bring us into oneness with him in every way. The darkness is not dark to him, and the night is as clear as the day (see Psalm 139:12).

REFLECT

Where do you feel stuck in your life? What does Jesus want to say to you and show you in this?

_____

_____

_____

_____

_____

_____

_____

_____

_____

_____

_____

_____

_____

_____

_____

_____

_____

_____

_____

_____

_____

_____

_____

_____

PRAY

_JESUS, I AM STUCK IN WHAT SEEMS
LIKE A HOPELESS DARKNESS. PLEASE
LIGHT MY WAY SO THAT I CAN SEE
THE PATH BACK TO JOY, WONDER,
AND TRUTH._

THIRD WEEK OF ADVENT

FRIDAY

MAY YOUR GRACE, ALMIGHTY
GOD, ALWAYS GO BEFORE US
AND FOLLOW AFTER, SO THAT
WE, WHO AWAIT WITH HEARTFELT
DESIRE THE COMING OF YOUR
ONLY BEGOTTEN SON, MAY
RECEIVE YOUR HELP BOTH NOW
AND IN THE LIFE TO COME.

COLLECT FOR MASS OF THE DAY

YOUR GOODNESS
AS A CHILD

We come once again to our Friday recollection and we sit with the Lord. You may have noticed some places of pain in your heart this week regarding your childhood and being a child. Can you imagine yourself or find actual pictures of yourself as a child? Perhaps you can spend some time today looking at pictures of yourself as an infant, at two years old, or at seven years old. Would you be willing to spend some time with yourself when you were twelve, fifteen, seventeen years old?

Sometimes these pictures or memories bring happiness and smiles as we behold our innocence and call to mind the details of the event, the fun adventure of childhood, or a long-awaited vacation with our family or friends. Other times we cringe when we see ourselves at certain ages, for we know our vulnerabilities at that time. We remember the Christmas when certain things did or did not happen. We can often still feel in our body the reactions we had to certain people in the picture with us. The pictures tell us stories about parts of our heart that are still very much alive. And Jesus loves us in every single place.

On this Friday, Jesus desires to share with you about your goodness as a child and the truth of your heart. Would you allow Jesus to be with you here today and reveal to you whatever he would like to reveal? Jesus reveals these places with reverence and the truth of his love. May we allow him to speak to our hearts.

REFLECT

What were you like as a child? What would it be like to spend time with you when you were twelve, fifteen, seventeen years old?

_____

_____

_____

_____

_____

_____

_____

_____

_____

_____

_____

_____

_____

_____

_____

_____

_____

_____

_____

_____

_____

_____

_____

_____

_____

PRAY

*LORD JESUS, GRANT ME CLARITY
OF YOUR PRESENCE, THAT I MAY
HEAR YOU SPEAK THE TRUTH TO
MY HEART.*

SATURDAY

O WISDOM OF OUR GOD MOST
HIGH,
GUIDING CREATION WITH
POWER AND LOVE:
COME TO TEACH US THE PATH
OF KNOWLEDGE!

O ANTIPHON

THANKSGIVING AND
HEALING FOR OUR CHILDHOOD

God, thank you for the gift of being a child and for my childhood. Thank you for the eternal mystery and wisdom of these days, where you began to teach me the path of knowledge. Thank you for uniting my life to yours in my infancy, as a small child, as I grew and then became an adolescent. Thank you for the gifts of learning, growing, mastering skills, and exploring the world. Thank you for childhood friends, playing with joy, and learning in school and in life. Thank you for the goodness of my being small and receptive to your grace.

Jesus, you said to let the little children come to you, and to not prevent them, for the kingdom of God belongs to them (see Matthew 19:14). This is me, Lord, and today I entrust every moment and every memory of my childhood to you and I unite it to yours.

I also pray for healing for myself in the places where my childhood was painful. For the times when I felt lonely, unwanted, forgotten, or rejected, please heal me, Lord. Please heal me especially of . . . (*call to mind specific wounds*).

Please heal me from any bitterness that I may have toward myself as a child or about my childhood. (*Ask the Holy Spirit to bring to mind any resentments or judgments you may have toward yourself or prominent people from your childhood or any areas of unforgiveness.*) Lord, help me to be honest about these places and release these places to you, surrendering the outcome to you, knowing that you make all things new.

God, my Father, bless me in your power and love as your precious child. Jesus, please cleanse me with your precious blood, healing my heart and strengthening my love of you. Holy Spirit, may your healing love come upon me at this very moment. Thank you for guiding me.

Jesus, may I receive you anew as my Savior, Lord, brother, and friend. Open my heart with your gentle care. Show me how to love as you love, and set me free in your heart, in the joy that never ends.

Amen.

REFLECT

For what are you especially grateful regarding being a child and your childhood? What were some times you felt lonely, unwanted, forgotten, or rejected and for which you would like the Holy Spirit's help in finding forgiveness and healing?

_____

_____

_____

_____

_____

_____

_____

_____

_____

_____

_____

_____

_____

_____

_____

_____

_____

_____

PRAY

DEAR GOD, FOR MY CHILDHOOD AND THE WAYS YOU UNITED MY LIFE TO YOURS AS I LEARNED, MASTERED SKILLS, AND EXPLORED THE WORLD—THANK YOU. FOR THE PAINFUL PLACES IN MY CHILDHOOD WHERE I FELT LONELY, UNWANTED, FORGOTTEN, OR REJECTED—PLEASE HELP ME RELEASE THESE PLACES TO YOU, SURRENDERING THE OUTCOME TO YOU, KNOWING THAT YOU MAKE ALL THINGS NEW.

LORD GOD, FROM YOU EVERY FAMILY
IN HEAVEN AND ON EARTH TAKES ITS
NAME.

FATHER, YOU ARE LOVE AND LIFE.

THROUGH YOUR SON, JESUS CHRIST,
BORN OF WOMAN, AND THROUGH
THE HOLY SPIRIT, THE FOUNTAIN OF
DIVINE CHARITY, GRANT THAT EVERY
FAMILY ON EARTH MAY BECOME FOR
EACH SUCCESSIVE GENERATION A TRUE
SHRINE OF LIFE AND LOVE.

GRANT THAT YOUR GRACE MAY GUIDE
THE THOUGHTS AND ACTIONS OF
HUSBANDS AND WIVES FOR THE GOOD
OF THEIR FAMILIES AND OF ALL THE
FAMILIES IN THE WORLD.

GRANT THAT THE YOUNG MAY FIND
IN THE FAMILY SOLID SUPPORT FOR
THEIR HUMAN DIGNITY AND FOR THEIR
GROWTH IN TRUTH AND LOVE.

GRANT THAT LOVE, STRENGTHENED
BY THE GRACE OF THE SACRAMENT
OF MARRIAGE, MAY PROVE MIGHTIER
THAN ALL THE WEAKNESSES AND
TRIALS THROUGH WHICH OUR FAMILIES
SOMETIMES PASS.

THROUGH THE INTERCESSION OF THE
HOLY FAMILY OF NAZARETH, GRANT
THAT THE CHURCH MAY FRUITFULLY
CARRY OUT HER WORLDWIDE MISSION
IN THE FAMILY AND THROUGH THE
FAMILY.

WE ASK THIS OF YOU, WHO IS LIFE,
TRUTH AND LOVE WITH THE SON AND
THE HOLY SPIRIT.

AMEN.

**PRAYER OF ST. JOHN PAUL II
FOR FAMILIES**

FOURTH WEEK
OF ADVENT

THE HOLY
FAMILY

FOURTH WEEK OF ADVENT

SUNDAY

SHOWER, O HEAVENS, FROM
ABOVE,
AND LET THE SKIES RAIN
DOWN RIGHTEOUSNESS;
LET THE EARTH OPEN, THAT
SALVATION MAY SPROUT
FORTH,
AND LET IT CAUSE
RIGHTEOUSNESS TO
SPRING UP ALSO;
I THE LORD HAVE CREATED
IT.

ISAIAH 45:8

O LEADER OF THE HOUSE OF
ISRAEL,
GIVER OF THE LAW TO MOSES
ON SINAI:
COME TO RESCUE US WITH YOUR
MIGHTY POWER!

O ANTIPHON

JOURNEY WITH
THE HOLY FAMILY

This week as we prepare for the coming of the Son of God, we will journey with the Holy Family. Depending upon the calendar, this fourth week of Advent could have one day or six days, but we will spend them all with Jesus, Mary, and Joseph.

This week we journey with Mary and Joseph as they make their way to Bethlehem, where there will be no room for them at the inn. There they will settle in at a stable and Jesus will be born in humility in the quiet of the night. We will be with Mary and Joseph in the ordinary moments of life and in the extraordinary circumstance of God coming to earth as we all do, as a small and wonderful child.

The stable wherein Jesus is born says so much about the desires and love of God. It is no coincidence that Jesus is born in a stable. In the divine providence of God, he chooses to be born there. This act is rich in symbolism of many things, but I would like to offer a quote often attributed to Servant of God Dorothy Day for your pondering today and this week: "My soul is so much like a stable. It is poor and in unsatisfactory condition because of guilt, falsehoods, inadequacies, and sin. Yet I believe that if Jesus can be born in a stable, maybe he can also be born in me."

What we have noticed in our hearts these past three weeks is that we all have places of glory and places of poverty. As we consider our mothers and fathers and ourselves as children, we see the darkness and the light. We also see that Jesus is in the middle of everything. He desires to take us into his own family. Jesus desires to restore our families and our image of family. He reveals his glory in the very midst of our poverty, including the poverty of our families. It is here that Jesus decides and delights to be born again and again. It is right here, dear friends.

Oh, how he loves us. How deeply so.

May these days of Advent heal you and your family.

May the grace of these days heal mother, father, and child.

May these days lead to deep levels of grace, peace, understanding, kindness, newness, and compassion.

May you know that you are not alone on this journey and that Jesus, Mary, and Joseph are with you always, now and forever.

Amen.

REFLECT

What are places of glory and places of poverty within your heart that have been revealed to you over the last three weeks? How would you describe your image of family?

PRAY

*ALMIGHTY GOD, AS I JOURNEY
WITH THE HOLY FAMILY THIS FINAL
WEEK OF ADVENT, MAY I MINE THE
PLACES OF GLORY AND THE PLACES
OF POVERTY IN MY LIFE FOR THE
ETERNAL TREASURES OF YOUR LOVE.*

FOURTH WEEK OF ADVENT

MONDAY

O ROOT OF JESSE'S STEM,
SIGN OF GOD'S LOVE FOR ALL
    HIS PEOPLE:
COME TO SAVE US WITHOUT
    DELAY!

O ANTIPHON

A SIGN OF GOD'S LOVE

Each person and each family are called to be a particular revelation of God. Each family is called to image the Holy Family— father, mother, child together as a living unit of life-giving love. Each person and each family are called to be a sign of God's love. The beautiful truth about God is that he is sovereign and that all time belongs to him. There is not a moment in your life or in the life of another person wherein God is not present. And since God is present, he can bring healing to any aspect of our lives. We can ask him to heal our hearts, heal other people where we have wounded them, and heal our families.

Jesus comes to save us without delay. He understands family dynamics. No matter what your family looks like today or what it has been in the past, Jesus would like to come today in a new way to bring restoration, light, hope, and peace. What would you like Jesus to do for you?

REFLECT

As you look back upon your life or upon the family God has given you now, what are some aspects of your family that reflect God's plan? Where in your family do you see love lacking? Where do you need an encounter with the love of the Holy Family?

_____

_____

_____

_____

_____

_____

_____

_____

_____

_____

_____

_____

_____

PRAY

*LOVING FATHER, PLEASE HEAL
MY HEART AND THE HEART OF MY
FAMILY, AND RESTORE US AS A LIVING
UNIT OF LIFE-GIVING LOVE.*

FOURTH WEEK OF ADVENT

TUESDAY

O KEY OF DAVID,
OPENING THE GATES OF GOD'S
  ETERNAL KINGDOM:
COME AND FREE THE PRISONERS
  OF DARKNESS!

O ANTIPHON

THE KEY THAT
OPENS EVERY DOOR

Jesus Christ is the way (see John 14:6). With Jesus, there is always a way. He is the key that opens every lock and every door. He is the way through to freedom and life. Jesus desires for us and for our families to have life abundantly (see John 10:10), not to merely exist or survive. Living in Christ is true freedom. The only way that we can help heal broken family dynamics and continually foster healthy family dynamics is for us to personally allow Jesus to come and heal us every day. We must allow the Lord to bring to light all the areas of our lives that lead us away from him and from one another.

We often want other people in our family to change their ways. We sometimes believe that our personal holiness and growth is dependent upon whether other people in our family change their behavior, beliefs, and the like. We often believe that they need to change first and then we will do so. Although changes in the behavior of our family members can certainly help change the dynamics of our family for the better, the only person we can directly bring into the realm of transformation with Jesus is ourselves.

We must, dear friends, be very honest with the Lord about the places that need his healing in our personal lives, and we must ask for the grace and courage to take the next step forward in this process of transformation. Can we ask Jesus today to reveal places where we are prisoners of darkness, so his light can come and purify our sins, falsehoods, and unholy attachments? Can we ask him to come and clean the stable of our souls? Advent is an important time of year for us to make a good confession in the Sacrament of Reconciliation and begin again with the light of his grace. The more we do this, the more it changes our families for the better, for the truth of God's love begins to permeate our souls, emanating outward toward all whom we encounter.

REFLECT

Where in your life could you especially benefit from Jesus's purifying light to cleanse your sins, falsehoods, and unholy attachments?

_____

_____

_____

_____

_____

_____

_____

_____

_____

_____

_____

_____

_____

_____

_____

_____

_____

_____

_____

_____

_____

PRAY

*JESUS, THERE ARE PLACES IN MY LIFE
WHERE MY BEHAVIOR, BELIEFS, AND
THE LIKE HOLD ME A PRISONER OF
DARKNESS. MAY YOUR LIGHT PURIFY
MY SINS AND CLEANSE THE STABLE
OF MY SOUL.*

FOURTH WEEK OF ADVENT

WEDNESDAY

O RADIANT DAWN,
SPLENDOR OF ETERNAL LIGHT,
  SUN OF JUSTICE:
COME AND SHINE ON THOSE
  WHO DWELL IN DARKNESS
  AND IN THE SHADOW OF
  DEATH.

O ANTIPHON

THE BEAUTY OF STILLNESS

There is something deeply wonderful about the radiance of dawn in the stillness of the morning. The splendor of the quietness of the rising sun and the promise of a new day shines upon the deepest places of our hearts. The beauty of stillness has the power to disarm us and to remind us of what matters most.

When we think of family at Christmastime, it can stir up a lot within us. Perhaps we have distinct memories of Christmas that were beautiful, loving, warm, joyful, hope-filled, and fun. Perhaps we also have distinct memories of Christmas that were sorrowful, isolating, fear-filled, or disappointing. Jesus understands all of that.

Mary and Joseph would have had a mix of feelings within as they traveled to Bethlehem and as it became apparent that there was "no place for them in the inn" (Lk 2:7) to rest for the evening and for Mary to give birth to the Savior of the world. The deep simplicity of the stable and the manger was the providence of God and a saving grace for you and me. In the simplicity, in the darkness, Jesus, the light of the world, is born.

We often have a lot of expectations of Christmas and of ourselves and our families during this time. Of course we want things to be joyful and happy, and that is a beautiful and good desire. But shall we ask the Lord to reveal the places where we have expectations that might be pressing out the very joy and happiness we are seeking? Can we ask Jesus to show us the places he is inviting us to simplicity, peace, and rest? Let us ask him for the grace to surrender all our hopes and desires so he can give us the gift of his very self.

REFLECT

What are some Christmas expectations that may be overshadowing Advent's call to simplicity, peace, and rest? How might you ask Jesus to help you reevaluate those expectations to better embrace the spirit of Advent and what matters most?

PRAY

*JESUS, HELP ME SURRENDER MY
EXPECTATIONS FOR CHRISTMAS SO
THAT I CAN ENCOUNTER THE TRUE
SOURCE OF HAPPINESS: SIMPLICITY,
PEACE, AND REST IN YOUR PRESENCE.*

FOURTH WEEK OF ADVENT
THURSDAY

O KING OF ALL NATIONS AND
KEYSTONE OF THE CHURCH:
COME AND SAVE MAN, WHOM
YOU FORMED FROM THE
DUST!

O ANTIPHON

GOD'S PLAN FOR YOUR FAMILY

Each one of us is a unique, precious, and unrepeatable creation of God. We are incomparable to one another in the gift of who we are because we are each a particular manifestation of the glory of God, never before revealed to the world. The sacredness of each human life is stunning to behold. We are made by God, we came from God, and we are going back to him. God has no other purpose in creating us other than to reveal his goodness and to bring us into his own blessed life (*CCC* 1).

God searches us; he knows us. All of our ways are open before him; he knows every part of our being. He knit us together in our mother's womb, and we are fearfully and wonderfully made (see Psalm 139:14). God also knows every member of our family. He knows them through and through, and he has gifted each of them to us and us to them.

Families are a great mystery. It's likely that we have each wondered at times as to why God put us in our family or why he placed certain people within our family. What was and is his plan for each member of our family and for our family as a whole? Families are not an accident, nor the result of mere chance. Each family is particularly crafted and thought out by God. No matter what has happened in our family, be it deep sorrow or deep joy, God has a plan in it all.

REFLECT

Have you ever considered God's plan for your family? How might you ask God to reveal his plan for your family?

_____

_____

_____

_____

_____

_____

_____

_____

_____

_____

_____

_____

_____

_____

_____

_____

_____

_____

_____

_____

_____

_____

_____

PRAY

*ALMIGHTY GOD, HELP ME TO
CELEBRATE EACH MEMBER OF MY
FAMILY AND OUR FAMILY UNIT AS A
WHOLE AS SACRED AND BEAUTIFUL
MANIFESTATIONS OF YOUR GLORY.*

FOURTH WEEK OF ADVENT

FRIDAY

O EMMANUEL, OUR KING AND
GIVER OF LAW:
COME TO SAVE US, LORD OUR
GOD!

O ANTIPHON

AWAITING WITH ANTICIPATION

It is almost time to celebrate the arrival of our Lord and King. We can imagine what this last day was like for Mary and Joseph as they arrived in Bethlehem amid the crowds of people. We can imagine the stirring of the baby Jesus in Mary's womb as Joseph astutely looked for a safe place for her to give birth.

We can imagine the truth of the extraordinary in the ordinary, as much of our lives feel like this. God comes to us in extraordinary ways in the most ordinary of moments. It is amazing to think that no one in Bethlehem had any idea of what was about to happen. No one in that town knew that the King of kings was about to be born among them in the most ordinary and impoverished place. Mary and Joseph probably interacted with many people during those days, and all the people they beheld only saw a young pregnant woman and her devout husband leading a donkey. No one saw the Radiant One in the womb of the beautiful woman. No one knew the truth of the man to whom God had entrusted his own Son to. Such hiddenness. Such ordinariness. Such is the way of God.

Perhaps these days in our homes we are awaiting with anticipation the ones who have loved us our whole lives and who are deeply embedded into our stories. No one has any idea of the impact they have made upon us or the gift they have been to us. They are extraordinary in their ordinariness. They are cherished and held dear, and we cannot imagine life without them. Even in the sorrowful places, God makes whole and transforms dread into true anticipation. In the heart of the newborn Savior, all is seen, understood, and made whole. All can be made new.

REFLECT

Who in your life would you describe as extraordinary in their ordinariness? How have they affected your life?

_____

_____

_____

_____

_____

_____

_____

_____

_____

_____

_____

_____

_____

_____

_____

_____

_____

_____

_____

_____

_____

_____

_____

_____

PRAY

*GOD, AS I ANTICIPATE THE ARRIVAL
OF YOUR SON, I MARVEL AT THE WAYS
YOU BRING THE EXTRAORDINARY
TO EVEN THE MOST ORDINARY AND
IMPOVERISHED PLACES IN MY LIFE.*

FOURTH WEEK OF ADVENT

SATURDAY

FOR TO US A CHILD IS BORN,
TO US A SON IS GIVEN;
AND THE GOVERNMENT WILL BE
UPON HIS SHOULDER,
AND HIS NAME WILL BE CALLED
"WONDERFUL COUNSELOR, MIGHTY
GOD,
EVERLASTING FATHER, PRINCE
OF PEACE."
OF THE INCREASE OF HIS
GOVERNMENT AND OF PEACE
THERE WILL BE NO END,
UPON THE THRONE OF DAVID, AND
OVER HIS KINGDOM,
TO ESTABLISH IT, AND TO
UPHOLD IT
WITH JUSTICE AND WITH
RIGHTEOUSNESS

FROM THIS TIME FORTH AND
FOR EVERMORE.
THE ZEAL OF THE LORD OF HOSTS
WILL DO THIS.

ISAIAH 9:6-7

BORN IN YOU

God with us. God with his creation. God with his children. God with his family. In the profound workings of God, he answers the plea of humanity for a savior, for reconciliation, for salvation. We come now to the moment of the most wondrous birth in the history of creation. Jesus Christ, the King of the kings, comes to be with us. He comes to reconcile all things to himself (see Colossians 1:20). Every aspect, every moment, of our lives is surrounded by the nearness of God. He has never left us for a moment. He is with us. He is the answer to every question we have and every happiness we seek. It is Jesus.

In the quiet of this night, he is born in the stable of your heart and in the stable of your family. He comes gently, honorably, reverently, lovingly. He comes as a child, just as you did. He comes born of a woman, just as you were. He comes with a heavenly and earthly father, just as you did. Jesus comes to make all things new.

We celebrate his birthday today and during this Christmas season. We celebrate and rejoice in the grace and truth of the reconciling of our lives, our families, this world. No matter what your life looks like at this time, commend your life to Jesus and ask him to bring you his peace, light, and truth. No matter what your family looks like at this time, commend it to Jesus and ask him to bring your family healing, understanding, and joy. He is in the stable with you, and you are in the stable with him. You are loved, and with Jesus, you are home.

Welcome home.

Merry Christmas.

REFLECT

How would describe your family at this time? In what areas could your family especially benefit from Jesus's healing love?

_____

_____

_____

_____

_____

_____

_____

_____

_____

_____

_____

_____

_____

_____

_____

_____

_____

_____

_____

_____

_____

_____

_____

_____

PRAY

JESUS, MAY NOT ONE OF MY DAYS
BE WITHOUT YOUR PEACE, LIGHT,
AND TRUTH.

SR. MIRIAM JAMES HEIDLAND, SOLT, is a popular Catholic speaker, cohost of the *Abiding Together* podcast, and the author of the bestselling books *Loved as I Am* and *Restore: A Guided Lent Journal for Prayer and Meditation*.

A former Division I athlete who had a radical conversion and joined the Society of Our Lady of the Most Holy Trinity in 1998, Heidland has shared her story on EWTN's *The Journey Home*, at numerous SEEK and Steubenville conferences, and at the USCCB's Convocation of Catholic Leaders.

In addition to speaking, Heidland has served in parish ministry and as the director of novices for her SOLT community. She also has served as an assistant to both her provincial and general superiors.

Heidland earned a master's degree in theology from the Augustine Institute and speaks extensively on the topics of conversion, authentic love, forgiveness, and healing.

JOSIAH HENLEY is a Catholic illustrator and designer from Portland, Oregon.

He earned a master's degree in architecture from Portland State University. His work is inspired by the ancient art and architecture of the Church, and aims to create contemporary images that honor her tradition.

He lives with his family in Portland, Oregon.

https://heartofiesvs.etsy.com
Instagram: @heartofiesvs

Free *Behold* companion resources and videos
are available to enhance your Advent experience
and make it simple to customize for individual use or
for use in parish, small groups, or classroom settings.

Visit **avemariapress.com/private/page/behold-resources**
or scan the QR code below to find

- weekly companion videos with
  Sr. Miriam James Heidland, SOLT,
- *Behold Leader's Guide*,
- pulpit and bulletin announcements,
- downloadable flyers, posters,
  and digital graphics,
- and more!